SHIRE NATURAL H

CW00971645

THE PUFFIN

JIM FLEGG

CONTENTS

The Puffin 2
Puffin colonies 6
The Puffin's year 10
Past and present problems 19
Watching Puffins 23
Further reading 24

Series editor: Jim Flegg.

Published in 2001 by Shire Publications Ltd, Cromwell House, Church Street,
Princes Risborough, Buckinghamshire HP27 9AA, UK.
Website: www.shirebooks.co.uk
Copyright © 1985 by Jim Flegg.
First published 1985; reprinted 2001.
Number 2 in the Shire Natural History series. ISBN 0 85263 744 6.

Printed in Great Britain by CIT Printing Services Ltd,
Press Buildings, Merlins Bridge, Haverfordwest, Pembrokeshire SA61 1XF.

The Puffin

The handsome and charming Puffin, elegant in black and white plumage resembling a dinner jacket, is one of the most popular of birds, fascinating both the experienced ornithologist and the man in the street. Its clown-like face, multicoloured beak and quizzical expression are well known, but the Puffin remains one of the more difficult birds to study in detail. Its comings and goings are notoriously fickle, and it nests in a burrow often too deep and too dark to permit its egg or young to be seen, and where it is relatively intolerant of disturbance. From these depths, adult birds incubating their single grubby white egg can be heard producing grumblings and groanings and the most extraordinary of sepulchral moans.

Puffins are seabirds—exclusively so, for those that do occasionally occur inland, for example on reservoirs, are invariably sickly or, more often, storm-driven birds seeking any refuge in extreme circumstances. They are members of the auk family, the Alcidae, often called Alcids for short, which occupy in the colder-water zone of the northern hemisphere much the same sort of niche as do the penguins, which are unrelated, in the southern hemisphere. Like the penguins, Alcids are clumsy on land because their feet are placed so far back on the body, and, again like the penguins, all are excellent swimmers. There are, however, considerable size differences between the two families, as the largest of the Alcids is not much bigger than the smallest of the penguins.

The Alcids include auks, guillemots, razorbills, auklets, puffins and murrelets, all of which are small or more often medium-sized birds rather stout in the body and with relatively small wings. Though Alcid wings are reduced in size to improve their under water swimming efficiency, only in the case of the recently extinct Great Auk has this reduction produced a flightless bird, and nowhere has the adaption been as extreme as the stiff paddles that serve the penguins for wings. In flight, although they are reasonably fast, their short wings do not allow much manoeuvring capability, and the Alcids are characterised by direct flight, on whirring wings, usually low over the water. When landing on the sea, Puffins sometimes seem just to stop flying a few inches above the waves, landing with a brick-like splash and sometimes submerging briefly before bobbing buoyantly up to the surface. In strong cross or tail winds, landings at the burrow entrance or on the cliff face may also prove difficult, requiring several circuits in flight before the final attempt is made at landing. Even so, undignified tumbles and somersaults are not infrequent in these conditions. On land, like the penguins, they more often than not adopt an upright stance unless resting or incubating an egg.

Alcids come to land during the summer months to breed, usually choosing remote coastlines and islands, though they may occasionally visit their colony areas during spells of fine, calm and mild weather in winter. For the rest of the year most are maritime, spending their time in flocks often not very far from land, though to this the Puffin can be an exception, occurring in mid Atlantic.

There were twenty-three Alcid species, of which one, the Great Auk *Pinguinis impennis,* also the largest, is now extinct, the last specimens having been slaughtered during the second half of the nineteenth century, one of the consequences of flightlessness. The Great Auk was confined to the North Atlantic Ocean and the abutting areas of the Arctic Ocean, and the same is true of the Razorbill *Alca torda,* the Puffin *Fratercula arctica* (sometimes called the Common or Atlantic Puffin), the Little Auk or Dovekie *Plautus alle* and the Black Guillemot *Cepphus grylle.*

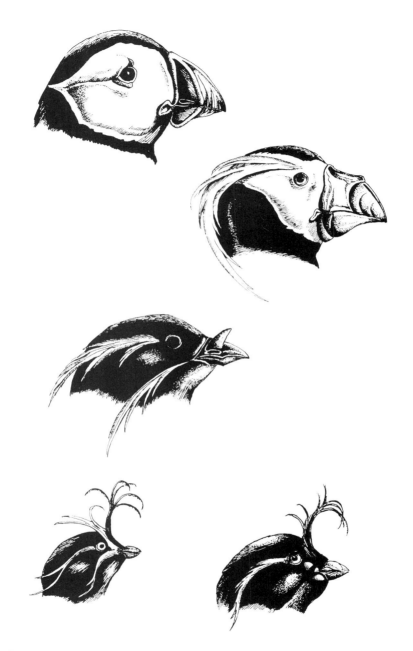

Top left, Common or Atlantic Puffin; top right, Tufted Puffin; centre, Rhinoceros Auklet; bottom left, Whiskered Auklet; bottom right, Crested Auklet.

3

Two other Guillemots or Murres, Brunnich's *Uria lomvia* and Common *Uria aalge*, occur in both Atlantic and Pacific oceans, but the remaining members of the auk family, the considerable majority, are essentially Pacific Ocean birds.

In summer the plumages of most Alcids are predominantly black above and white below, though there are exceptions like the Black and Pigeon Guillemots. In winter, both black and white tend to become shades of grey, and the demarcation lines between two become blurred. Such plumage coloration or elaboration as does occur is most marked in the puffins and the auklets. The parrot-like red, yellow and blue-grey beak of the Atlantic Puffin in summer is well known, and its Pacific counterpart the Horned Puffin, sports a beak of similar size and shape, but only in red and yellow. More elaborate is the Tufted Puffin, with an orange beak with a green base, and with a large drooping tuft of yellow feathers stretching over each eye and down on to its shoulders. The smaller Rhinoceros Auklet has a yellow 'horn' on its beak and blue drooping 'eyebrow' feathers, while the Whiskered and Crested Auklets, both also Pacific birds, have the most extraordinarily elaborate fountain-like tufts of black and white feathers sprouting from their crowns.

The Atlantic Puffin stands about 1 foot (30 cm) tall, with a wingspan of about 18 inches (45 cm). It is portly in build, and in summer jet black above, pure white below. The head is black save for a large heart-shaped white patch on each side. The eye is large and dark, surrounded by a red ring, and above it is a blue-grey horny triangle, below it a similar small rectangle. Of all its features the beak is the most remarkable. Huge, often as deep as the head itself, it is compressed laterally. In profile it is reminiscent of a parrot's beak with a rounded upper mandible and a slightly hooked tip. The basal area is pale blue, the area near the tip red, with a yellow band separating the two and a fleshy, crinkled yellow patch at the 'hinge'. The orange-red legs are short and strong, for burrow digging: the feet, of a similar conspicuous colour are webbed and armed with sharp dark claws ⅜ inch (1 cm) long. The red portion of the beak has vertical grooves, which increase in number and length with age: an adult in breeding condition will probably have two complete grooves and be about five years old.

In winter there are considerable changes. Black areas become greyer, the white underparts are less pure, and the face patches become smoky grey. The horny patches and eye-ring are shed, and the yellow wattle at the base of the beak shrivels. More remarkably, the basal blue-grey part of the beak is shed and the red area becomes greyish yellow, so the profile becomes distinctly different, with the beak considerably slimmer from top to bottom and appearing longer and more like that of a Razorbill. Youngsters that have fledged in late summer resemble winter adults with smoky grey faces and even more slender dark grey beaks.

Puffins are commonly pictured with a beak full of fish, held sideways. Popularly, they are said to hold their prey in neatly alternating fashion, first a head, then a tail, and so on. Reality is not so precise but, unusally, the number of fish in their catch often exceeds the popular belief that they can hold even ten or a dozen small fry crosswise! A beak containing only a few large fish, like sand eels, probably indicates that fishing conditions are good and that young will be well fed, while a load of perhaps fifty or sixty small fry (even higher numbers are on record) is indicative of poor fishing and hungry young.

How they hold so many fish and how they catch them so neatly in the first place are intriguing questions to most people. How they catch them is not known, and to find out would demand underwater observations that would be extremely difficult to carry out at a range at which their technique would be clearly seen without disturbing the Puffin or its prey. It is however, possible to answer anatomically the question of how they are held. Both mandibles of the beak are sharp-edged, and the palate or roof of the mouth is well provided with large, sharp, backward-pointing projections, all helping to hold slippery prey. Moreover, the jaws of

RIGHT: *An adult Puffin in summer, when the cheeks are white and the various horny or fleshy head ornaments are present. These, and the size, shape and colours of the beak itself, are thought to be associated largely with display, not feeding.*

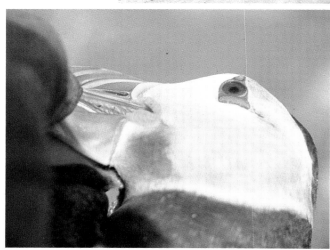

LEFT: *The roof of the Puffin's mouth, its palate, is well provided with sharp, backward-pointing projections. These help keep secure a beakful of small, slippery fish, held against them by the Puffin's stiff tongue. The edges of the beak also play a part: they are sharp and the jaw muscles are strong, hence the hand holding the beak open is gloved for protection.*

birds in general, and of Puffins in particular, do not have a simple hinge as in the mammals, including man. Between the upper and lower jaws, instead of a rolling joint, the Puffin has a short stout bone, the quadrate, which allows the beak to open in a double-jointed, wide-gaping fashion, and for the upper and lower madibles to be kept parallel as the mouth opens, with their fish-gripping adaptations still functioning.

The other skeletal adaptations of the Puffin are concealed beneath its covering of feathers. The feathers are smooth and close-packed, covering a downy layer which, holding air, serves as effective thermal insulation. For seabirds, feather care is of vital importance, and Puffins spend much time preening to keep their plumage in good condition. The feathers are water-repellent and maintained so by regular applications of 'preen oil' from a gland situated just above the tail. So effective is this waterproofing that not only are Puffins buoyant swimmers but when they dive they take with them a silvery air bubble, sheath-like round their bodies. It is when they dive to hunt that these other skeletal adaptations come into play.

Most birds have many fewer vertebrae in their backbones than comparable mammals, and those that they have are often fused together. In addition, their pelvis (or rather pelvic girdle) is large and robust and usually fused to the vertebrae. Such is the case with the Puffin, where the backbone forms a short stout rod. The breastbone, or sternum, is similarly strong. It has a deep keel with the wing muscles situated on either side, the whole providing an excellent shock absorber for the Puffin's not infrequent poor landings on either the sea or the land. Between these two strong elements are the ribs, and the cage that they form must protect all the vital organs of the Puffin (save those in its head) from the pressures exerted by the sea during dives. The ribs are fused at each end to the backbone and the sternum, and the rigidity that this gives is further enhanced by unusually long uncinate processes. Uncinate processes are an avian skeletal speciality: they are antler-like processes protruding backwards from each rib like a flattened branch, arising about midway down the rib and extending to overlap one (sometimes two) adjacent ribs, to which they are firmly held by connective and muscular tissue. In the Puffin, this 'box girder' structure is unusually strong and ideally adapted to the birds' way of life.

Puffin colonies

Although during the winter months the occasional Puffin may be seen almost anywhere in the coastal seas surrounding Britain and Ireland, during the summer the vast majority of Puffins will be in the vicinity of their breeding colonies, or puffinries. Colonies are in remote, almost inaccessible places, often on islands uninhabited by man, in the north, especially in the Orkneys and Shetlands. Although present in the past in some numbers, they have today almost gone from the English Channel coast, while in the east suitable cliffs only from Flamborough Head northwards support colonies. There are more puffinries on the western, generally rocky, shoreline of Britain and Ireland, and numbers are higher there, tending to increase towards the north.

Much detailed knowledge of Puffin distribution was obtained by a special seabird survey, Operation Seafarer, organised by the Seabird Group in 1969, the results of which were published in *The Seabirds of Britain and Ireland* (Cramp, Bourne and Saunders, 1974), and from the fieldwork between 1968 and 1972 leading to the publication by the British Trust for Ornithology of *The Atlas of Breeding Birds in Britain and Ireland* (edited by J. T. R. Sharrock, 1976). Maps in these two books show a

RIGHT: *A Puffin beak opening with the mandibles parallel. The quadrate bone at the jaw 'hinge' is shaded darker and shaped like an upside-down letter 'Y'.*

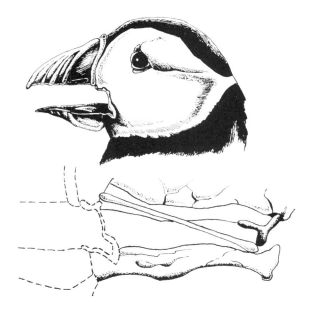

BELOW: *Top left, a nestling; top right, a breeding adult; bottom left, a year old in summer; bottom right, an adult in winter.*

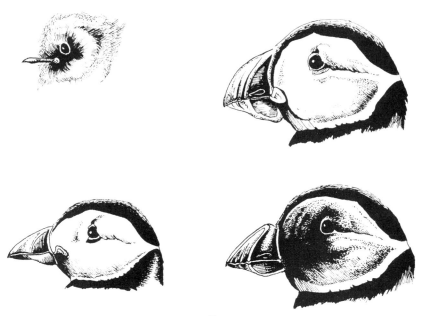

7

The grassy slopes of Dun, St Kilda, are riddled with burrows. Each burrow mouth is marked by trampled vegetation, scorched brown by the birds' excreta.

heavy concentration of major colonies in the north and north-west of Britain. The related Razorbill and Guillemot were each recorded as breeding in about 10 per cent of the approximately 3800 ten kilometre squares of the National Grid covering Britain and Ireland, their distributions being geographically very similar with heavy emphasis on the west coast from Cornwall to Cape Wrath. In contrast, in western Ireland Puffin colonies are considerably fewer and further apart , and only from the Isle of Skye northwards do they appear nearly as densely placed as the other Alcids. It is no surprise, therefore, that the *Atlas* showed Puffins breeding in only 6 per cent of the squares. There are intriguing numerical anomalies here, though. Operation Seafarer set out to provide population estimates for seabirds, acknowledging the difficulties in obtaining accurate or even comparable counts for behaviourally awkward species in difficult terrain for taking a census. The Guillemot emerged as the most numer-

ous seabird in Britain and Ireland, at 577,000 pairs, while the Razorbill, though similarly distributed, was in much smaller numbers at 144,000 pairs. In contrast, the Puffin, seemingly scarcer than both, came second to the Guillemot (and ahead of the Herring Gull and Kittiwake) at 490,000 pairs.

Roughly one third of the confirmed breeding records of Puffins came from offshore islands rather than mainland coasts, and this and the relative absence of Puffins from the south and west coasts of England and Wales—areas well frequented by holidaymakers—perhaps indicate that Puffins are more sensitive to human disturbance than other auks. They may be more subject to disturbance because of their preference for founding colonies on grassy slopes, many of which are capable of supporting sheep throughout the summer. The feet of the sheep may destroy nesting burrows, or the shepherds may disturb the breeding birds, but if this is the case it becomes difficult to understand the sta-

8

ABOVE: *A group of Puffins loafing on the Farne Islands. Before the egg hatches, there seems to be plenty of time for such gatherings in calm weather.*

BELOW: *Carn Mor is a precipitous boulderfield, several acres in extent, on the southern coast of Hirta, St Kilda. Puffins (and other seabirds) nest deep in the cavities between rocks.*

bility of colonies on remote islands—all well stocked with sheep of necessity—when these islands or their near neighbours were inhabited during the eighteenth and nineteenth centuries.

Most puffinries are large, and many enormous, with tens or even hundreds of thousands of pairs. Some occur in holes in sea cliffs, particularly smaller colonies such as at Bempton in Humberside or at Portland Bill in Dorset. Others occur in the extensive screes and boulder tumbles that are often found at the head or the foot of such cliffs. One of the most spectacular of these is that on Carn Mor, on the southern coast of Hirta, the main island of the St Kilda group, lying out in the Atlantic some 45 miles (72 km) west of the Outer Hebrides. At this point the cliffs are precipitous and spectacular, rising almost 1000 feet (300 m) from the sea. Carn Mor is reached by descending terrifyingly steep grassy slopes. At a distance, it looks like any other scree, but, on closer approach, its real magnitude can be assessed when it is no longer dwarfed by the towering cliffs. It is several acres in extent, and some of the boulders are the size of a large room! In the tunnels and cavities beneath and between these boulders, tens of thousands of Puffins share the shelter with (probably) similar numbers of Storm and Leach's Petrels. If it is difficult to take a census of Puffins in such terrain, the problems of counting black-plumaged petrels, also burrow nesters but only visiting their colonies in any numbers on moonless nights, are much greater.

More usually though, Puffins nest in burrows in the grass swards at the top of the cliffs, although these colony types intermingle depending on the terrain, as on the Inner Farne, off the Northumberland coast, or on Dun in the St Kilda group. The Puffins may themselves dig these burrows in the soft, often dry soil beneath the turf, making use of the long sharp claws on their strong feet, or they may commandeer them from rabbits or Manx Shearwaters. The grassy slopes are usually covered in pink thrift, white sea campion and often bluebells, all flourishing on the guano deposited by the seabirds and forming an attractive

backdrop to the social gatherings at burrow entrances and communal flypasts that are so much a part of the Puffins' life.

The Puffin's year

In winter most Puffins will have dispersed widely from their breeding colonies and seem often to be found in ones and twos, not in large 'rafts' like the other auks. Some remain in the North Sea and in the Bay of Biscay, while a few penetrate into the Mediterranean. Puffins remain further out to sea than Guillemots or Razorbills, and perhaps the majority will spend the winter scattered over the North Atlantic, possibly feeding largely on plankton. Even the juvenile birds may be far ranging; two nestlings ringed on St Kilda, off the Outer Hebrides, were recovered during the following winter over the Newfoundland Banks. Results of studies of recoveries of ringed birds are considered later. Because of their remoteness, and the difficulties in conducting observations in winter in the North Atlantic, there is still a great deal to be discovered about the ecology of Puffins at this time.

Birds may arrive back at their colonies occasionally on fine warm days in late February, but usually it is not until March and April that their attendance is regular. At first they tend to come and go quickly or spend much of the time in restless rafts offshore. Sometimes the majority may vanish out to sea for several days. From all appearances, many of the birds seem to be paired on arrival (colour-ringing studies support this view), but despite this a great deal of display occurs, both in the rafts on the sea and among those birds that venture ashore to the colony areas. As the season advances, so more and more time is spent ashore, in displaying and in

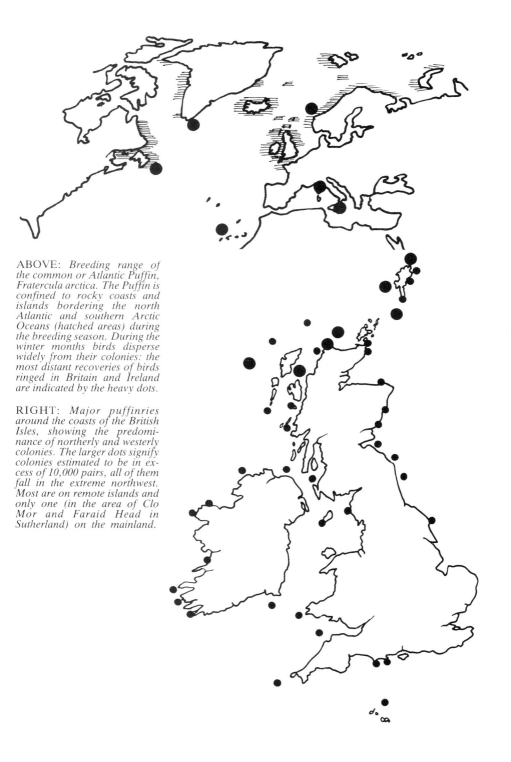

ABOVE: *Breeding range of the common or Atlantic Puffin, Fratercula arctica. The Puffin is confined to rocky coasts and islands bordering the north Atlantic and southern Arctic Oceans (hatched areas) during the breeding season. During the winter months birds disperse widely from their colonies: the most distant recoveries of birds ringed in Britain and Ireland are indicated by the heavy dots.*

RIGHT: *Major puffinries around the coasts of the British Isles, showing the predominance of northerly and westerly colonies. The larger dots signify colonies estimated to be in excess of 10,000 pairs, all of them fall in the extreme northwest. Most are on remote islands and only one (in the area of Clo Mor and Faraid Head in Sutherland) on the mainland.*

ABOVE: *Gatherings ashore are notoriously fickle in occurrence. Early in the season, fine calm days will often result in a steadily growing group, as will days of thick sea mist, such as this on Great Saltee.*

BELOW: *Offshore gatherings, in rafts at the foot of the cliffs, are also irregular except on calm days early in the season. Then, most serious display takes place on the water, as does its culmination in copulation, when the female is almost submerged as the male mounts her back, wings flapping.*

ABOVE: *Newly-arrived Puffins gathering at their colony on the island of Skokholm.*

BELOW: *At the start of each season, established birds and newcomers alike indulge in a ritual (and for the new pairs, practical) inspection of burrows, to establish their state of repair and whether they are occupied. At this time the two sexes can often be distinguished, the male having an appreciably larger head.*

seeking or renovating a nest burrow.

Display between Puffins can best be described as 'billing and cooing', with a great deal of gentle head and neck nibbling between the pair, sometimes accompanied by a muted crooning. When they are together, the male is just discernibly larger, particularly his head, than the female. The male makes ritual presentations of bits of grass and feathers, potential nest material, to the female, and the two in close company prospect several burrows. If digging must be done, both birds participate and the bird not working stands near the burrow entrance, often getting showered in the dirt excavated, with powerful kicks, by its mate. Other ritualised movements are seen, including head tossing or jerking to attract attention, or perhaps as a gesture of appeasement, and a downheld beak indicative of aggressive intent, a posture adopted to repel invaders without actual battle. Often these displays and burrow investigations are interrupted by inquisitive neighbours, and the courtship degenerates into a brawl. The general promiscuity evident at this time earned the Puffin its colloquial French name of 'mormon'. Results of detailed studies suggest, however, that such promiscuity is more apparent than real and that Puffins have a relatively strong fidelity to their mates.

As old burrows are claimed or new ones dug, occasional squabbles develop. At this stage of nest building and peak display, Puffins are at their most vociferous. Considering that their voice is restricted to a low growl, the range of emphasis that they achieve, from the erotic to the enraged, is remarkable. Copulation is most often seen on the sea just offshore below the colony. In mid May (rarely earlier but often later, until mid June) the single egg is laid in a chamber at the end of the burrow, which may be 2 yards (2.2m) or even longer, or part of a honeycomb with other occupants like shearwaters, petrels or rabbits in side branches. The nest chamber is often lined with a little dry grass or a few feathers, sometimes with some freshly gathered greenery.

The single egg is white in colour, chalky in texture and relatively large.

Close inspection shows that many of them have faint brown specklings, which are quickly lost under a coating of dust or mud. Every so often a heavily marked egg is found and these markings may imply that Puffins once nested in the open, like Razorbills and Guillemots. Occasionally clutches of two eggs are reported, though it is extremely difficult to be sure that these are the product of a single female. There are other suggestions that the Puffin once produced two-egg clutches (like the Black Guillemot often still does): for example, it has two 'brood patches', one on each side of its breast bone. These brood patches are areas of naked skin, well supplied with superficial blood vessels, which warm the egg during incubation, the breast feathers serving as an insulating surround.

The egg is incubated by both parents, in shifts, for about six weeks. It hatches to reveal a chick densely clad in fluffy down, almost black above and grey below. As it also has dark eyes and a tiny dark beak, finding it must be difficult for the adult, returning with food and plunging into a dark burrow from the bright sunlight outside. The youngster grows rapidly in normal circumstances, fed on fish of a variety of sizes from hatchlings to fully grown and of a variety of species. Studies by Dr M. P. Harris published in 1978 compared Puffin foods on St Kilda and on the Isle of May in the Firth of Forth. Generally, Puffins fed their young on the most abundant mid-water fish in the vicinity, but they did show some selectivity. When available, sand eels and sprats were by far the most important prey, while rockling and whiting, though taken, were less suitable because of their size and their poor calorie content as food. Other fish like flatfish or young gadoids were only occasionally taken.

In some years Harris found that the St Kilda birds fed their young almost entirely on whiting, but in these years their fledgling weights (and thus probably also their chances of survival) were lower than usual. Differences in available fish prey (sand eels are common around the Isle of May) may in part explain the

14

Puffins will usually nest at the top of cliffs. If they dig their own burrows they share the work in mated pairs, the partner not working standing near at hand.

differing circumstances of these two puffinries, with St Kilda apparently just stable after a severe decline in numbers, while the Isle of May colony is rapidly increasing in size. It is difficult to extrapolate from the food of the young what the diet of the adults contains. Remains from various dead birds examined indicate that sand eels feature prominently, but that various pelagic worms and shrimps, as well as other crustaceans, are also eaten.

During the breeding season Puffin attendance at the colonies varies enormously, even at the height of the season. When they are ashore, the Puffins spend considerable periods standing around resting and preening, and occasionally displaying or fighting. Attendance is reduced once the egg is laid, the off-duty partner being busy feeding out at sea ready for its spell on the egg, and numbers on shore are frequently low

until the chicks hatch. Often, though, Puffins come up on to the cliffs in large numbers before stormy or wet weather, during sea fogs or on exceptionally fine calm days.

Most feeding visits by parents to young occur early in the morning and they become fewer during the day, with perhaps a small increase again in the late afternoon. The growth of the chick varies, depending on place, food and weather, but usually about fifty days elapse between hatching and fledging. Towards the end of this period, the chick in a good year has plenty of fat, and feeding visits may be fewer and at longer intervals. Usually, however, the chick is fed until the day it leaves the nest.

Fledging is a hazardous process, with predatory gulls always on the alert for an unsuspecting young Puffin. Departure is after dark, following a couple of evenings spent by the young Puffin standing,

LEFT: *Though several dozen small fry are on record in a single beakful, a load of a few large fish such as these sandeels is far more nutritious for the young. Normally, birds returning with a load of food head for the safety of their burrows as quickly as possible, but non-breeders may 'practise' fish catching and loiter about the colony carrying a beakful.*

BELOW: *The 'midden' of corpses (mostly Puffins) close by the nest of a pair of Puffin-eating-specialist Great Black-backed Gulls on St Kilda. Such pairs can cause considerable mortality and chaos over a small area.*

ABOVE: *A Herring Gull waiting to intercept a home-coming Puffin carrying a load of food for its young on Great Saltee. Other Puffins, though not involved, stand around clearly uneasy in the background.*
BELOW: *A ringed Puffin. One leg carries the standard metal alloy serially-numbered British Trust for Ornithology ring, the other a plastic laminate ring with an engraved individual letter code. These letter codes can be read at a distance with binoculars or a telescope, and have proved a great aid in studies of longevity and burrow and mate fidelity.*

or wing exercising, at the mouth of its burrow. Moonless nights are safest, as the goal of the young Puffin is to get as far out to sea as possible by daylight. It may be some weeks later that the last adult departs. The young Puffin will not return to the colony for at least a year, and it seems that perhaps the majority of young do come back to their natal colony or close to it. For the first two or three years of their life, they undergo a wing moult which leaves them flightless, or nearly so, during the spring, delaying their return until summer is well advanced. As they grow older, so they return earlier to the colony, and at the age of four or five they begin to participate more in its life, beginning to display and prospect for a mate and a burrow.

Besides providing information on migratory routes and dispersal to wintering areas, ringing recoveries give some indication both of causes of death and of mortality rates. The recoveries must be analysed with caution, as they are open to many biases (like the improbability of the recovery of any birds that die in mid Atlantic, so that neither their age nor their cause of death features in the overall analysis if it differs from those of birds recovered from inshore waters and in close proximity to man). Even so, these recoveries do offer some indications worthy of mention: in an analysis of recoveries from the major European ringing schemes published in 1984, Dr Harris found that the recovery rate was much lower than that for other auks at less than 1 per cent, which suggests that Puffins winter further out to sea than Razorbills, Guillemots and Black Guillemots. In the light of Puffins' pelagic behaviour, ringing recoveries seem unlikely to reveal much about either migration routes or wintering areas.

An earlier analysis by C. J. Mead, published in 1974, suggested that the survival of adult Puffins from year to year could be as high as 90 or even 95 per cent, and 90 per cent would approximate to the results of studies of individually colour-ringed Puffins at their breeding colonies. As they have a high fidelity to both mate and burrow from year to year, colour-ringed birds returning to colonies

are perhaps the best material from which to assess mortality or survival. Of Puffins ringed as chicks and later recoverd (there are only about two hundred such recoveries, so too much faith should not be placed in estimates derived from such a sample), Harris assessed a 25 per cent mortality or thereabouts, in each of the first two years (counting the year of birth as the first), 19 per cent in the third year and 8 per cent in the fourth and fifth.

Both Mead, who was dealing soley with Puffins ringed in Britain and Ireland, and Harris agree that to put too much faith in the recorded causes of death could also be misleading. The majority of ringed Puffins recovered are 'found dead' and the finder offering no suggestion as to the cause. These amount to about 80 per cent of total recoveries, and for the remainder there are three paramount causes of death: oiling, shooting and being caught in fishing nets. The prevalence of each of these three categories varies depending on where in the North Atlantic the birds were found. Oiling predominates in the North Sea, the English Channel and the Bay of Biscay; being trapped in fishing nets prevails off western Britain and Ireland, and to a considerable extent also in the west Atlantic and off the Scandinavian Coast; while shooting seems to be the major identified cause of death off Scandinavia, Spain and Portugal, north-west Africa and (to a lesser degree) off the Canadian coast. Such figures largely reflect what is known about nations which shoot auks for food (as others shoot wildfowl), about the increased likelihood of pollution in the North Sea and its approaches, and about where fishing activity is greatest.

When it comes to winter dispersal away from the breeding colonies, and bearing in mind biases due to lack of mid ocean recoveries, considerable differences are apparent in the distribution of ringing recoveries from various parts of Britain and Ireland. Least mobile are Puffins breeding on the east coasts of Scotland and northern England. The vast majority of recoveries from these colonies are within the North Sea basin, with a few south to Biscay, a few across in Scandinavia and a few to the north in the Orkneys, Shetlands and Hebrides. Birds from colonies in northern Scotland tended to be at rather greater distances: a few were in the North Sea basin, the majority in the Bay of Biscay. A handful had penetrated into the Mediterranean, and there were scattered distant recoveries from Greenland, Newfoundland, the Canary Islands and Madeira. Birds ringed in western Wales and Scotland and in Ireland apparently wander far more. Though recoveries are plentiful off the western seaboard of the British Isles, there are many in the Bay of Biscay and around the Iberian peninsula, and several in the Mediterranean as far east as Sicily (the longest recovery so far on record, from St Kilda, a distance of about 2500 miles [4000 km]). Almost as far flung are recoveries from north-west Africa, from the Canaries, and again from Newfoundland and south Greenland. Just as spectacular are recoveries of Icelandic-ringed Puffins in Newfoundland (many), the Bay of Biscay and the Azores, indicating that northerly breeding birds may winter well to the south. As with a number of other birds, Puffins in their first year seem to disperse over greater distances than when they are older.

Past and present problems

Assessing past levels of Puffin populations and any changes in them is particularly difficult because of the lack of any remotely accurate census figures. Depending on the distance back in time, we are forced to rely on narrative accounts and, more recently, surviving photographs of thriving colonies. On such evidence, Puffins would appear to have been more numerous, perhaps considerably more numerous, in the past than at present. There is, however, also reasonable evidence, at least from the recent

past, that sudden declines may be a feature of the Puffin's history. On Lunday, in the Bristol Channel, often called the 'Isle of Puffins', it is thought to have been the accidental introduction (with household food or furniture) of the devastating brown rat that caused the decline of a once flourishing colony to a few hundred pairs. Not far away to the north, on Grassholm (off south-western Dyfed) a colony estimated at half a million pairs may have become extinct at its own hands—or rather feet. As on many maritime islands, the soil on Grassholm was very organic and friable: here the birds may have burrowed to such an extent that the thin layer of soil over the rock became honeycombed. Wind and water combined as erosion forces during the winter to strip off the soil, leaving only the bare bedrock that now carries a spectacularly huge gannetry.

Local declines and increases are to be expected in any bird populations: alarm should be generated only when these declines are huge and difficult to explain. The history of the Puffin on St Kilda, the Puffin's acknowledged stronghold in Britain and Ireland, since the eighteenth century provides a wide-ranging account of the various pressures on the birds and how they have reacted to them. In the regrettable absence of detailed figures, the accounts of early writers visiting this remote island group (an adventure in itself even today, far more so in the past) cannot be ignored entirely. Macaulay, writing in 1765 of his stay on the islands, says: 'incredible flights of these Puffins flutter, during the whole summer season, round about St Kilda and the two isles pertaining to it: sometimes they cover whole plots of ground, and sometimes while on the wing, involve everything below them in darkness, like a small cloud of locusts in another country.' The Rev. Mackenzie, resident cleric to the small community on St Kilda between 1829 and 1843, estimated that 'there can be no less than three million of them' and recorded an annual 'harvest' during this period of eighteen to twenty thousand birds killed for food and feathers. Sands, writing in 1878, having spent a whole summer on

The old Village Street on Hirta, St Kilda. Seabirds, Puffins prominent amongst them, were vital in the past to the livelihood of remote island communities like St Kilda. Catches were shared fairly amongst families, and as much as possible was stored for winter consumption. Eggs were buried in charcoal, and adult birds slit open and dried, rather like herrings, for later consumption.

the islands, calculated that during his stay 89,600 Puffins had been killed.

In the past seabirds formed an important element in both the diet and the economics of isolated maritime communities, from the north of Scotland to the Arctic and in some areas they still do. Two Puffins are reputed to make a man-sized tasty meal in the Faeroe Islands, and the Eskimos consider a blubber-lined seal skin stuffed with un-gutted and unplucked Puffins, left over-winter to 'mature', to be a delicacy. Feathers and down, having good insulating properties, were even used to pay the rent in kind to the laird or landlord.

Such is the confiding nature of Puffins that they can be approached, with some caution, and hooked round the leg with a miniature shepherd's crook, and then pulled swiftly to hand to be killed. Fleyging, netting birds in flight with a giant butterfly net as they wheel over the cliff edge, was a dangerous but high-yielding occupation, which is still pursued in the Faeroes and elsewhere. The first few birds were caught and killed, and then positioned in lifelike postures around the fowler to lure other Puffins within netting range.

Against this background, it is difficult to understand the stability in the past of puffinries on remote islands like St Kilda, where for centuries the Puffin fulfilled this vital role in the human economy. Each year many thousands, sometimes apparently as many as 100,000, were slaughtered, 'harvested' for food. Some were eaten immediately, others split open and salted or dried for consumption during the winter, when protein-rich food would be scarce. There were no long-term drops in numbers, and it seems that the good husbandry of the islanders, taking a strictly rational 'crop' that they knew the population could sustain, ensured this. It is evident that the islanders considered the possible impact of what they were doing and even prevented the over-exploitation of 'easy' catching areas (and the over-provisioning of certain favoured families) by allocating egg-collecting and fowling sites on the island to different families on a yearly rota.

Towards the end of the nineteenth century the Kearton brothers, the pioneer Victorian natural history photographers, visited St Kilda, participating in most of the islanders' occupations and taking many photographs, which form a valuable historical archive. They recorded kills of up to 620 Puffins in one day by a man with a rod and noose and were graphic in describing their impressions of the obviously huge number of birds. They said of Hirta and Dun: 'here the Puffins breed in immense numbers, and the clouds of birds that swept past us made a sound like a whirlwind whipping up a great bed of dead rushes'; and of Soay, 'Puffins simply swarmed in the air . . . on the rocks . . . and dotted the sea all around as far as the powers of a pair of good field glasses could make them out.' Heathcote, writing in 1900 about a complete summer he and his sister spent on these remote islands, makes similar comments: 'absolutely bewildering, the never ending stream of birds passing by' and 'the slopes of Dun . . . are honeycombed by their burrows'.

More recent visiting naturalists, more concerned with science than spectacle, can only echo descriptions of this nature. They found estimating Puffin numbers (until the 1960s) such a daunting task that most avoided the issue, but estimates ranging from hundreds of thousands to about three million pairs were suggested by ornithologists familiar with large seabird colonies.

It might have been expected that with the withdrawl of the small human community on Hirta, forced by adverse conditions and ill health to request evacuation in the 1920s, the St Kilda Puffin population would have slowly expanded as hunting pressures were removed. There seems to have been little discernible change before 1960, but the Operation Seafarer census visits in 1969 and subsequent years revealed dramatic changes.

Many areas rich in Puffins in earlier photographs were now deserted, and numbers had diminished considerably. For example, on Dun the reduction continued during the survey years until only the seaward tip of the island held any quantity. Elsewhere, the slopes of the islands, so often photographed packed with Puffins, were deserted. The vegetation was rank, mostly dominated by sorrel growing vigorously on guano deposited over previous centuries. Closer examination showed that these slopes were still riddled with burrows, but deserted ones, with cobwebs covering their entrances. The total number of burrows was estimated to be not very different from the estimates of of three million pairs, but censuses at the time suggested that only a few hundred thousand pairs remained on the islands.

The 'northwest quadrant' of the Atlantic coast of Scotland contains many large colonies, and the St Kilda situation was made the more disturbing by reports of major declines at several of them, including the Shiants in the Hebrides, Clo Mor on the Sutherland coast and

Finlay McQuien noosing Puffins with a rod and line on the slopes of Hirta, St Kilda, photographed by the Kearton brothers during their visit to the islands at the end of the nineteenth century. Puffins no longer breed in this area of the island.

Foula in the Shetlands. Although visiting these remote islands is difficult and taking an effective census there so much more so, it seems clear that Puffin numbers were dramatically reduced, probably largely during the 1960s. Some comfort can be derived from an apparent stability since the early 1970s of many of the affected colonies, and indeed some puffinries elsewhere, as on the Isle of May in the mouth of the river Forth, have even expanded in recent years, though these increases go only a little way towards redressing the earlier losses elsewhere.

What, then, are the pressures on modern Puffin populations? On land, their upright stance and waddling gait make them clumsy and render them very vulnerable to predation by Great Black-backed Gulls. These may pounce on unsuspecting birds loafing at their burrow entrance, or on hungry well grown chicks peering out anxiously to see whether the next meal is on the way. They may even chase and fly down the unfortunate Puffin in mid air, eating it, on occasion, whole and still alive. More often they will land and kill the Puffin with heavy stabbing blows from the beak, before turning it inside out to remove the skin and eating the flesh. Great Skuas will also attack Puffins, especially on the water, sometimes butchering whole rafts, which seem to do little to save themselves from the carnage. Seemingly less damaging are the attentions of Herring and Lesser Black-Backed Gulls. These are not often killers in the direct sense: usually they will wait near the burrow entrance for a bird attempting to return to its nest with a beakful of food for its young. This harassment, sometimes active and some-times relatively passive, has a disturbing effect on the Puffin, which may be forced to land some distance from its burrow or to 'crash land' nearby. In either case, the common outcome is that in the ensuing melee the load of fish is lost or grabbed and eaten by the 'kleptoparasitic' gull. Sometimes the gulls show extraordinary agility in leaping up to snatch the fish in mid air as the Puffin whirrs past over-head, but rarely will they chase Puffins in the air for any great distance.

In Britain and Ireland in general, and on St Kilda in particular, whilst this predation occurs, the population of pre-dators is so small that their influence on the Puffins, though gory, is insignificant on the population as a whole. This is true even though the nest of a pair of 'Puffin-specialist' Great Black-backs may be surrounded by a midden of the wings from perhaps a hundred Puffins. Elsewhere, for example in Newfound-land, kleptoparasitism has been shown to reduce materially the survival of young in some of the colonies studied.

In such an examination for possible causes, disease must be considered. It seems likely that any major epidemic among Puffins would occur while the birds were gathered at their colonies, giving the disease the maximum chance of spreading. Were this to be the case, the skeletal remains of dead birds would be expected in the burrows, but none were found on St Kilda.

More modern causes of wildlife population decline are often linked to pollution of some sort. For seabirds, the classical problem is oil, but oil-polluted Puffins do not feature commonly in beached bird surveys organised by the Royal Society for the Protection of Birds. This may be because oiled Puffins have unusual flotation properties and quickly sink, rather than washing ashore, or it may be that as they are more widely dispersed and further out to sea than other Alcids few oiled birds would reach the shore anyway. How-ever, their dispersal over such a wide area renders them less likely to be affected by wholesale winter plumage contamination.

The disposal of toxic chemical wastes in the seas and their subsequent fate is a problem whose study is still in its infancy, but research so far does not indicate high levels, in Puffin corpses, of major pollutants like the heavy metals and the chlorinated hydrocarbons, and it seems improbable that pollution of this nature is the basic cause.

One other major factor remains, though it is difficult to examine, let alone quantify, in retrospect. In the sea, as on land, there are climatic changes operat-ing in cycles often of many years dura-

22

tion. Changes in ocean currents, but particularly changes in sea temperatures in the Puffins' feeding grounds around the major colonies, would have a dramatic effect on fish populations, both in the numbers of fish available and in the variety of species involved. In the longer-term cycling of temperatures the peak was reached in the 1950s, which would have been a comparatively poor time for feeding as fish stocks would have been low. Since then, colder waters are prevailing and fish stocks increasing, perhaps accounting for the current stability in Puffin numbers. There is evidence from well studied Norwegian colonies that fish shortages in the vicinity can cause a dramatic fall in the numbers of young Puffins surviving.

Watching Puffins

Despite the evident hazards faced by Puffins, in the past typified by fowlers attempting to catch large numbers for food, even on the most inaccessible of remote islands, and at present by the increasing threats posed by pollution, it is still possible to see Puffins without undue difficulty.

The map of breeding colonies shows that Puffins are to be found, during the summer months, on many parts of the coast of Britain and Ireland. Encountering Puffins during the winter months is a matter of chance, as most are well out to sea, so this season should be excluded when planning expeditions. Furthermore, as for centuries past, most puffinries, particularly the larger ones, are in remote areas, exceedingly difficult of access for the vast majority of intending Puffin watchers. It can also be argued that the decline of Puffin populations along the south coast of England and in the Isles of Scilly is in some ways due to the Puffin's sensitivity to disturbance and mans ability to seek them out (with more leisure time, new motorways and

the like) and his growing enthusiasm for nature watching.

There are nevertheless several places where the Puffins are so used to regular visits by boatloads of enthusiasts that they have become perfectly tolerant of humans (providing that they behave reasonably), and other sites where the nature of the terrain gives the Puffins all the protection that they need from disturbance. Amongst mainland sites where Puffins can be safely, and reasonably easily, watched are the extreme tip of Portland Bill in Dorset, the RSPB reserves at Foulsheugh, north of Dundee, and Bempton cliffs, in Humberside between Scarborough and Bridlington. Most good puffinries for visiting are on islands, however, and these islands are usually either nature reserves or well served by local boatmen who are alert to the needs of both the Puffins and the tourists. Annet, in the Isles of Scilly, is one such, and others include Skokholm and Skomer, off south-western Dyfed; Great Saltee, off County Wexford; the Blaskets and Skelligs, off County Kerry; Handa, off Sutherland; Fair Isle, with its bird observatory, lying between the Orkneys and the Shetlands; the Isle of May, off Fife in the mouth of the Firth of Forth; and the Farne Islands, off Northumberland. Thus only for those living in east and south-eastern England are Puffins any great distance away.

Puffin watching requires very little specialised equipment. Most puffinries are subject to sudden changes in the weather and even in midsummer can be exposed and often cold and wet, so appropriate clothing should be carried however fine the day seems when you set out. Sea conditions can change for the worse, too, so have ample food with you. Because of the nature of the colonies or the shyness of the Puffins, a good pair of binoculars is an essential aid to relaxed and comfortable viewing. Cliffs and even seemingly innocuous grassy slopes are hazardous terrain and each year claim bird watcher's lives: they should be treated with the utmost respect. So, too, should the Puffins: even if you want to get just a little bit closer for a better view or a photograph, always put their interests first.

Those with the interests of Puffins at heart may well wish to pursue Puffin conservation or study even further. Puffin colony reserves are owned, amongst others, by the National Trust, the National Trust for Scotland, various regional or county Trusts for Nature Conservation and by the RSPB (the Royal Society for the Protection of Birds). The remit of the RSPB includes conservation through reserve ownership and by applying national and international political pressure (for example on pollution problems). For the Puffin watcher with more serious ideas of study in mind, the Seabird Group and the British Trust for Ornithology (BTO) offer a range of opportunities from taking censuses to bird ringing. Relevant addresses are listed below.

British Trust for Ornithology, The Nunnery, Thetford, Norfolk IP24 2PU. Telephone: 01842 750050. Website: www.bto.org

National Trust, 36 Queen Anne's Gate, London SW1H 9AS. Telephone: 020 7222 9241. Website: www.nationaltrust.org.uk

National Trust for Scotland, Wemyss House, 28 Charlotte Square, Edinburgh EH2 4ET. Telephone: 0131 243 9300. Website: www.nts.org.uk

Royal Society for the Protection of Birds, The Lodge, Potton Road, Sandy, Bedfordshire SG19 2DL. Telephone: 01767 680551. Website: www.rspb.co.uk

Seabird Group, c/o RSPB, The Lodge, Potton Road, Sandy, Bedfordshire SG19 2DL.

Further reading

Corkhill, Peter. 'Food and Feeding Ecology of Puffins', *Bird Study*, 20, 207–20, 1973.

Flegg, J.J.M. 'The Puffin on St Kilda, 1969-71', *Bird Study*, 19, 7–17, 1972.

Gibbons, David W., Reid, J.B., and Chapman, R.A. (editors). *The New Atlas of Breeding Birds in Britain and Ireland 1988–1991*. Poyser, 1993.

Harris, M.P. 'The Food of Young Puffins *Fratercula arctica*', *Journal of Zoology*, 185, 213–16, 1978.

Harris, M.P. 'Breeding Performances of Puffins *Fratercula arctica* in Relation to Nest Density, Laying Date and Year', *Ibis*, 122, 193–209, 1980.

Harris, M.P. 'Biology and Survival of the Immature Puffin *Fratercula arctica*', *Ibis*, 125, 56–73, 1983.

Harris, M.P. 'Movements and Mortality Patterns of North Atlantic Puffins as Shown by Ringing', *Bird Study*, 31, 131–40, 1984.

Harris, M.P. *The Puffin*. Poyser, 1984.

Holloway, Simon. *The Historical Atlas of Breeding Birds in Britain and Ireland: 1875–1900*. Poyser, 1996.

Kearton, R. *With Nature and a Camera*. Cassell, 1897.

Lloyd, Clare, Tasker, M.L., and Partridge, K. *The Status of Seabirds in Britain and Ireland*. Poyser, 1991.

Mackenzie, N. 'Notes on the Birds of St Kilda', *Annals of Scottish Natural History*, April 1905, pages 75–80; July 1905, pages 141–53.

Mead, C.J. 'The Results of Ringing Auks in Britain and Ireland', *Bird Study*, 21, 45–86, 1974.

Nettleship, D.N. 'The Breeding Success of the Common Puffin (*Fratercula arctica* L.) on Different Habitats at Great Island, Newfoundland', *Ecological Monographs*, 42, 239–68, 1972.

Sands, J. *Out of the World; or Life in St Kilda*. MacLachlan & Stewart, 1878.

Thom, Valerie M. *Birds in Scotland*. Poyser, 1986.

Acknowledgements

The author wishes to thank Julie Gibbs for producing the line drawings and his wife, Caroline, for her comments on, and typing of, the manuscript. All colour photographs were taken by the author and his wife. The photograph on page 21 is from the Kearton brothers' book *With Nature and a Camera*.